JOURNEYS

Program Authors

James F. Baumann · David J. Chard · Jamal Cooks
J. David Cooper · Russell Gersten · Marjorie Lipson
Lesley Mandel Morrow · John J. Pikulski · Shane Templeton
Sheila W. Valencia · Catherine Valentino · MaryEllen Vogt

Consulting Author · Irene Fountas

Common Core Consultants · Carol Jago · J. Helen Perkins

Unit 4

Unit 5

Unit 6

Fast Track

☑ **WORDS TO KNOW**
High-Frequency Words

is
how
of
so
many
where

Vocabulary Reader

Context Cards

Words to Know

Read Together

▶ Read the words.

▶ Talk about the pictures.

is

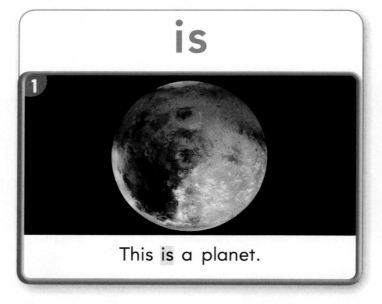

This **is** a planet.

how

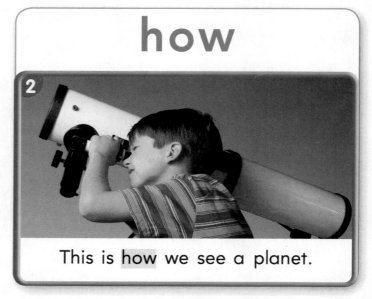

This is **how** we see a planet.

of

Earth is the name **of** our planet.

so

This spaceship is **so** big!

many

See how **many** stars there are!

where

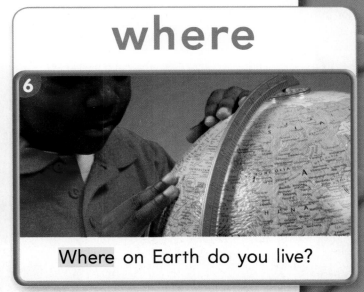

Where on Earth do you live?

Choose one word.
Use it in a sentence.

Your Turn

Talk About It!

What did you learn about science from the **Big Book?** Tell a partner.

my WriteSmart

Write About It!

Draw and write about what you would like to study.

I love volcanoes.

Cameron

 Go Digital

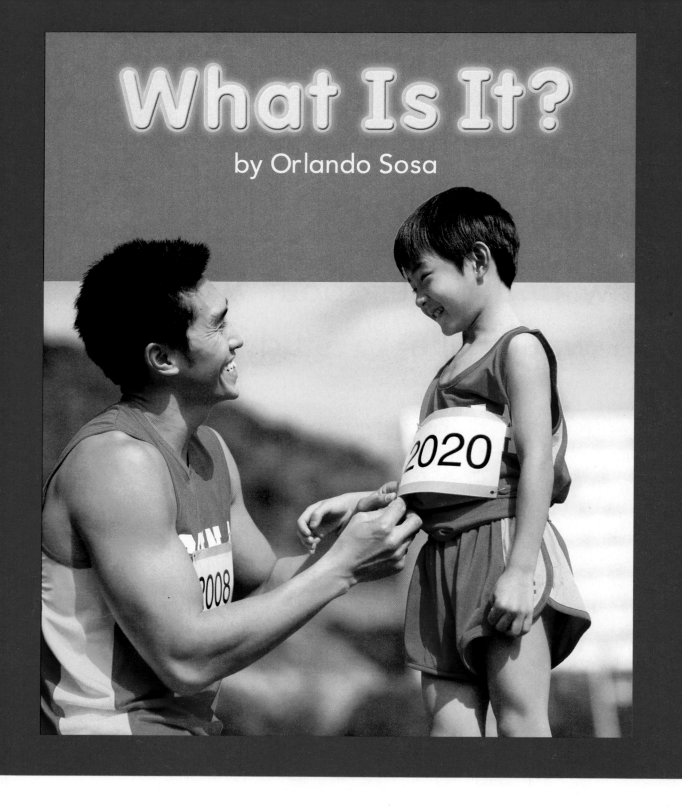

What Is It?

by Orlando Sosa

Tam can pin it. Pin, pin, pin.
What is it, Tam?

Pat bit it. Bit, bit, bit.
What is it, Pat?

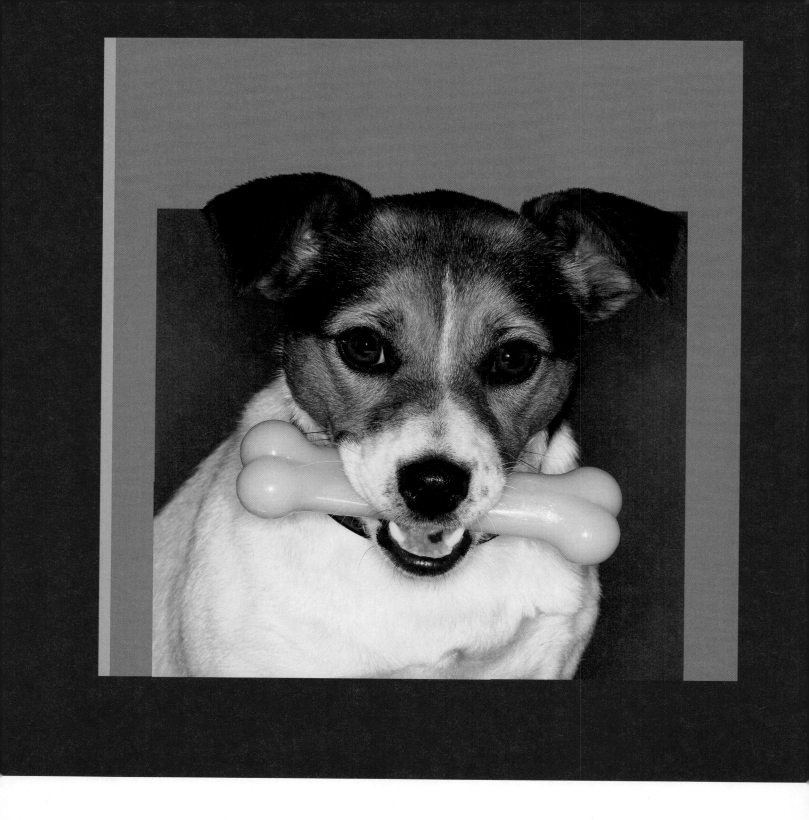

Sam can nip it. Nip, nip, nip.
What is it, Sam?

It can fit Cam. Fit, fit, fit.
What is it, Cam?

Tim can pat it. Pat, pat, pat.
What is it, Tim?

How can Pam see it?
Where is it, Pam?

Fit in My Cab

by Amy Miller-Krezelak
illustrated by Joe Boddy

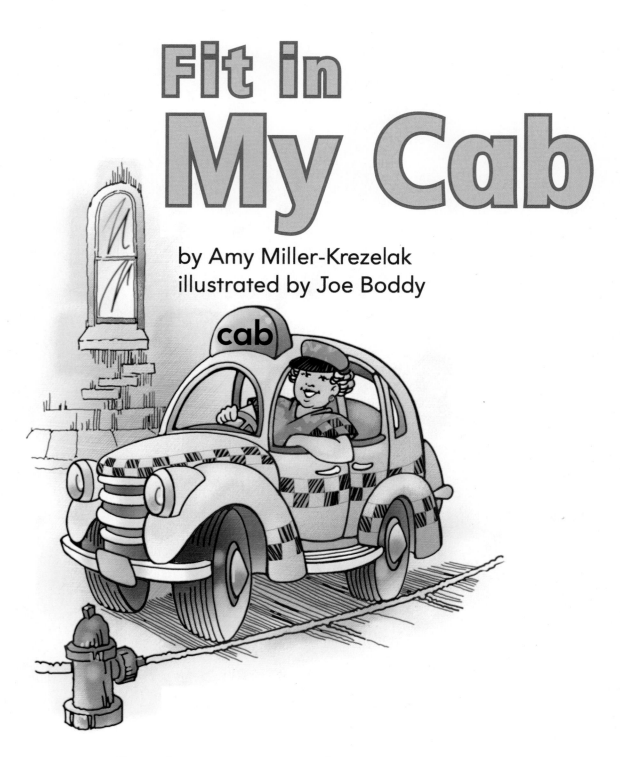

It is my cab.
I can fit in it.

Nat can sit in it.
Can Sam fit in it?

Sam can fit. Can Mac fit?
Mac can fit. Sit, Mac, sit!

How can Bab fit in it?
Bab can fit. Sit, Bab, sit!

Nat, Sam, Bab, and Mac can fit.
So, where can I fit in it?

Many can fit in my cab.

It is a bit of a fit in my cab.

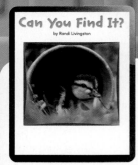
Can You Find It?
by Randi Livingston

Pam Pig
by Zev Herschel
illustrated by Liz Callen

☑ WORDS TO KNOW
High-Frequency Words

this

find

from

came

but

on

Vocabulary Reader

Context Cards

Go Digital

Words to Know

Read Together

▸ Read the words.

▸ Talk about the pictures.

this

1

Look at **this** big bug!

find

2

Can you **find** a bug?

from

The bee flew from flower to flower.

came

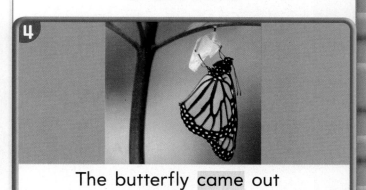

The butterfly came out of its chrysalis.

but

It doesn't look like it, but this will be a beautiful butterfly.

on

Do you see spots on the ladybug?

Choose one word.
Use it in a sentence.

Your Turn

Talk About It!

How do living things change as they grow? Talk to a friend about what you learned.

From Caterpillar to
BUTTERFLY
by Deborah Heiligman
Illustrated by Bari Weissman

Write About It!

Draw how a caterpillar becomes a butterfly. Label each stage.

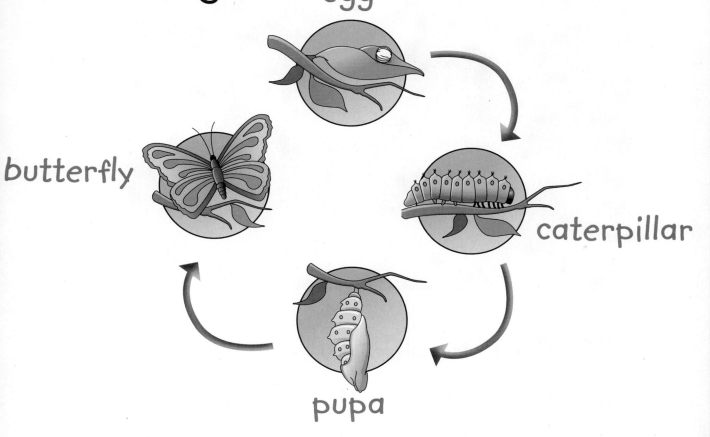

egg

caterpillar

pupa

butterfly

Go Digital

Can You Find It?

by Randi Livingston

Min can fit in this.
Min can sit in it. Find Min.

Tim can fit in this.
Tim can sit in it. Find Tim.

Pat can sit in this.
Pat can fit in it.

Sam can sit in the cap.
But the cap is big on Sam.

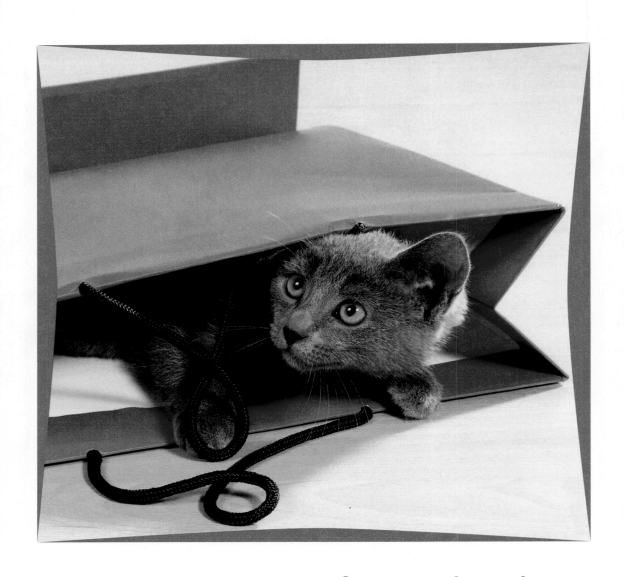

Tig can see me from this bag.
Tig can fit in it.

Nan can find Cam.
Tag! Now Cam is It!

Pam Pig

by Zev Herschel
illustrated by Liz Callen

This pig is Pam Pig.
Can Pam Pig find Pat Cat?

This cat is Pat Cat.
Can Pat Cat find Pam Pig?

Pam Pig sat.

Pam Pig came to find Pat Cat.

Pat Cat sat.

Pat Cat came to find Pam Pig.

Pam Pig came to see Pat Cat.
Pat Cat came to see Pam Pig.

Pat Cat can sit with Pam Pig.
Pam Pig and Pat Cat sat and sat.

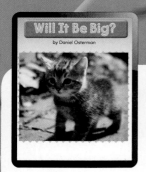
Will It Be Big?
by Daniel Osterman

Rip Is It
by Wendy Sinclair
illustrated by Diane Blasius

✓ **WORDS TO KNOW**
High-Frequency Words

will
be
into
that
your
who

Vocabulary Reader

Context Cards

RF.K.3c read common high-frequency words by sight

Go Digital

Words to Know

Read Together

▶ Read the words.

▶ Talk about the pictures.

will

We will look for a shark.

be

Fish can be great pets.

into

They all jumped into the water.

that

Can you see that whale?

your

Is your house near the ocean?

who

This is the man who fed the shark.

Choose one word.
Use it in a sentence.

Your Turn

Talk About It!

In what ways is the Atlantic Ocean special? Talk to a partner about it.

Write About It!

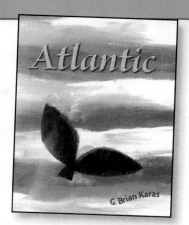

Atlantic

G. Brian Karas

Why is it important to care for oceans? Draw and write about it.

Fish need clean water.

Will It Be Big?

by Daniel Osterman

Tab! Tab! It is Tab.
Will Tab be big, big, big?

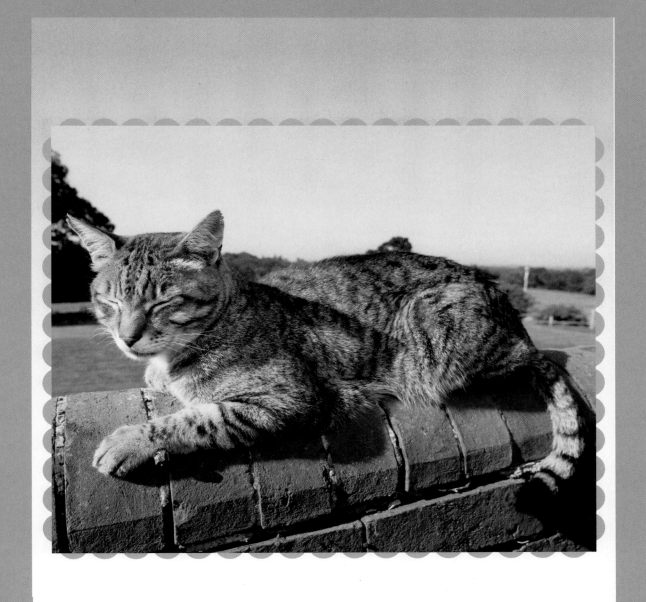

Tab will be big like your cat.
Big Tab can nap, nap, nap.

Who is that pig? It is Tim!
Will Tim be big, big, big?

Tim will be big, big, big.
Big Tim can sip it.

Cam! Cam! It is Cam.
Will Cam be big, big, big?

Cam will be big, big, big.
Big Cam can sit, sit, sit.

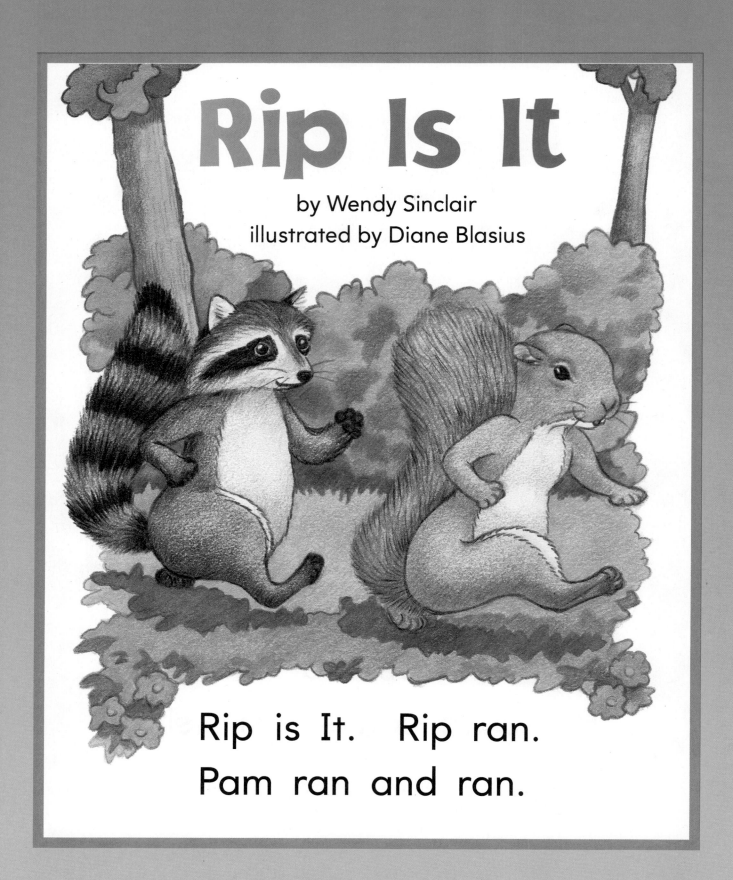

Rip Is It

by Wendy Sinclair

illustrated by Diane Blasius

Rip is It.   Rip ran.
Pam ran and ran.

Rip ran into Pam!
Rip can tag Pam.

Pam will be It now.
Can Pam tag Rip?

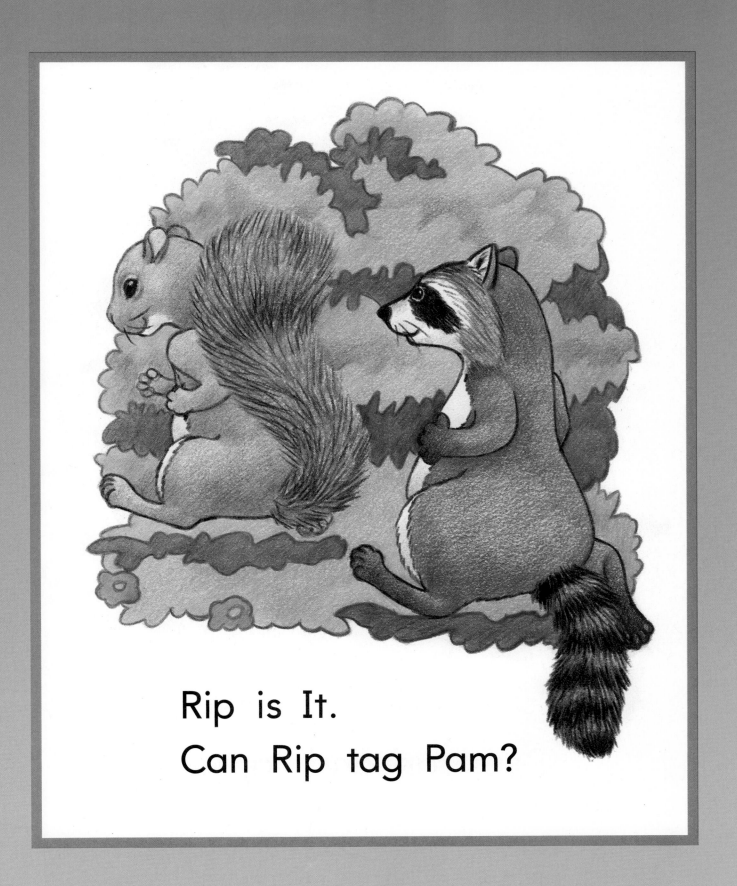

Rip is It.
Can Rip tag Pam?

Pam ran and ran.

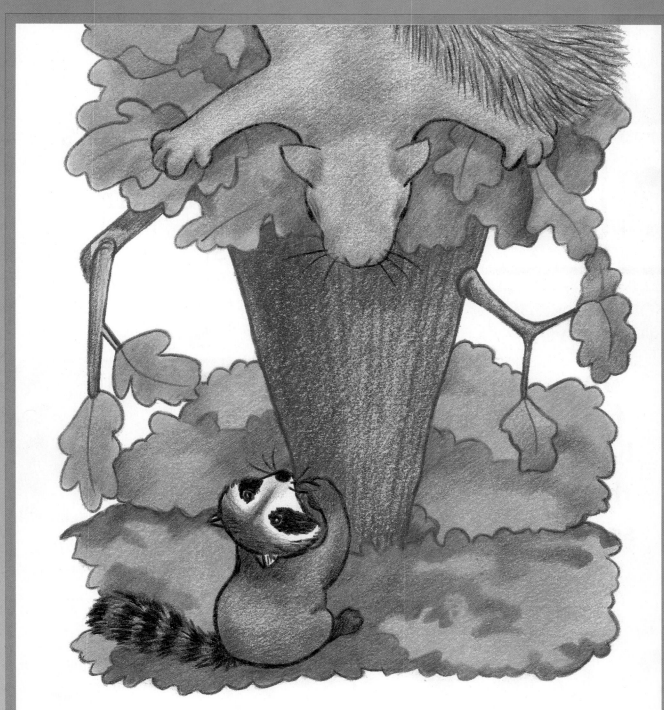

Can Rip tag Pam now?

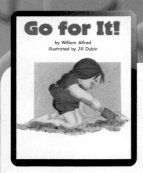
Go for It!
by William Alfred
illustrated by Jill Dubin

D Is for Dad
by David McCoy
illustrated by Lisa Thiesing

✓ **WORDS TO KNOW**
High-Frequency Words

go
for
here
they
soon
up

Vocabulary Reader

Context Cards

Going for a Hike
by Minnie Rolson
illustrated by Bob Masheris
HOUGHTON MIFFLIN

Go Digital

Words to Know

▶ Read the words.

▶ Talk about the pictures.

go

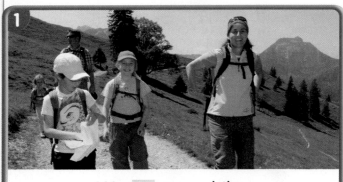
We **go** on a hike.

for

This backpack is **for** you.

58

here

We like to hike here in the hills.

they

They crossed the bridge.

soon

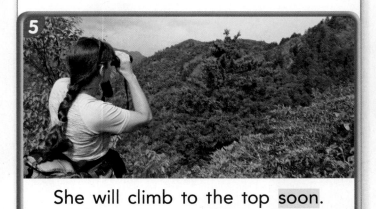

She will climb to the top soon.

up

They raced up the mountain.

Choose one word.
Use it in a sentence.

Your Turn

Talk About It!

What can happen on a hike?
Talk to a partner about it.
Use the **Big Book** for ideas.

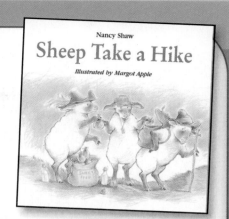

Write About It!

What part of the story do you like best? Why? Draw and write about it.

I like it when they find the path.

Go for It!

by William Alfred
illustrated by Jill Dubin

Here is Pat. Pat can dig.
Go for it, Pat!
Dig, dig, dig it, Pat.

Nan can dab.
Go for it, Nan!
Dab, dab, dab it, Nan.

Mim can sip it.
Go for it, Mim!
Sip, sip, sip it, Mim.

Dan can tap it for sap.
Go for it, Dan!
Tap, tap, tap it, Dan.

Sid can pat the big pig.
Go for it, Sid!
Pat, pat, pat the pig.

Tad and Pam can dip.
They go for it!
Dip, dip, dip, Tad and Pam!

D Is for Dad

by David McCoy

illustrated by Lisa Thiesing

D is for Dad.
Dad, dad. My dad is big.

D is for dig. Dig, dig, dig!
Dad Pig can dig it up.

Dad Pig can sit in a rig.
Dad Pig can dig it up.

Dad Pig is at bat.
Bat it, Dad. Bat it.

Dad Pig can go in for a dip.
Go for it, Dad!

D is for dad, my big dad.
Soon, I will be big like Dad!

The Big Dig
by David Michaels
illustrated by Robin Koontz

We Fit
by Cindy Evans
illustrated by Tim Bowers

☑ **WORDS TO KNOW**
High-Frequency Words

is
how
this
will
go
here

Vocabulary
Reader

Context
Cards

Curious About
the
Animal Park
by
Julius Richards

HOUGHTON MIFFLIN

This is a planet.

Go
Digital

Words to Know

Read
Together

▶ You learned these words.

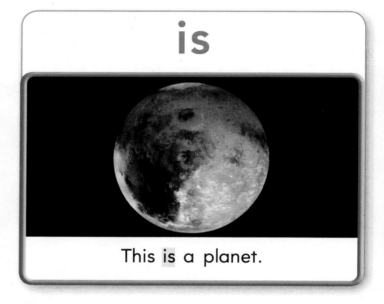

is

This **is** a planet.

how

This is **how** we see a planet.

this

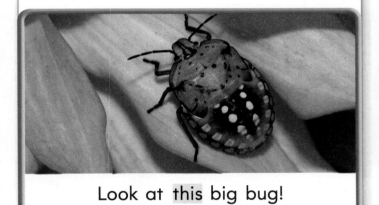

Look at this big bug!

will

We will look for a shark.

go

We go on a hike.

here

We like to hike here in the hills.

Now use each word in a sentence.

Your Turn

Talk About It!

How do scientists study dinosaurs? Talk to a friend about it.

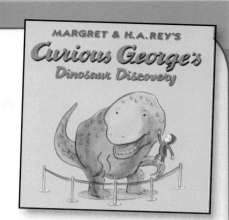

Write About It!

How does Curious George
find dinosaur bones? Draw
and write about it.

He dusts.

He digs.

The Big Dig

by David Michaels
illustrated by Robin Koontz

Pip will dig, dig, dig.
Pip will go find Sid.

Pip can rap, rap, rap.
Pip can tap, tap, tap.

Sid is in.
Pip did find Sid.

Pip can dig.
Sid can dig with Pip.
Pip and Sid dig and dig.

Tim can dig with Pip.
Tim can dig with Sid.
Tim, Pip, and Sid can dig.

Pip can pat it.
Sid can pat it.
Tim can pat it.
It is big!

We Fit

by Cindy Evans

illustrated by Tim Bowers

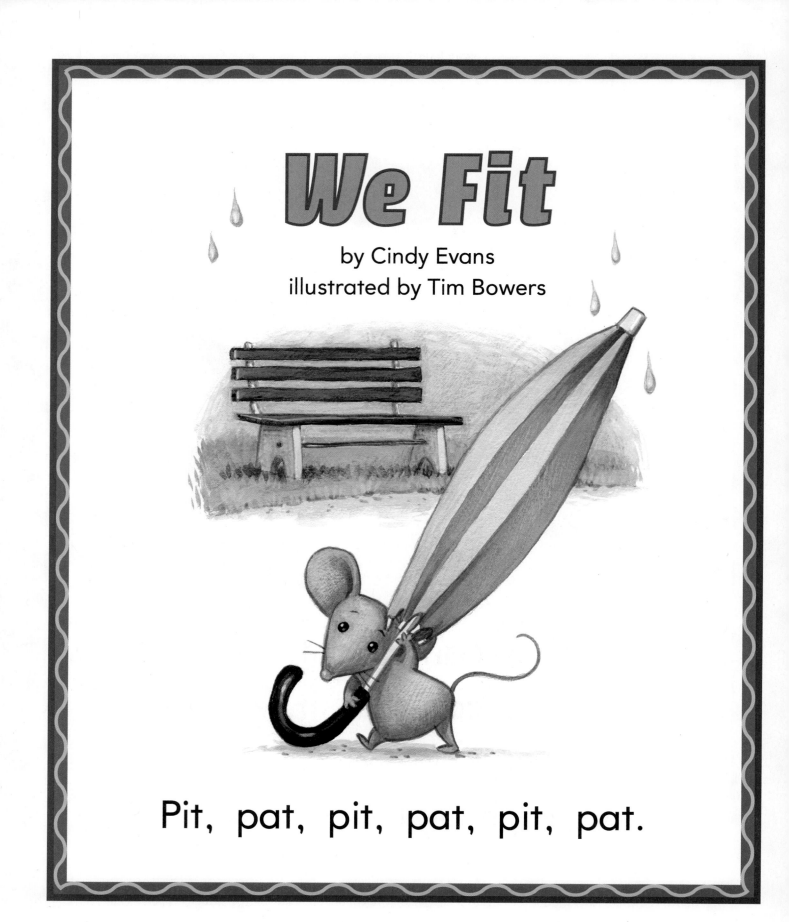

Pit, pat, pit, pat, pit, pat.

Pit, pat, pit, pat, pit, pat.
Sid can sit here.
Sid can fit.

Pit, pat, pit, pat, pit.
Can Sam fit here?
Can Sam sit with Sid?

Pit, pat, pit, pat, pit.
Can Rib fit here?
Will Rib, Sam, and Sid sit?

Pit, pat, pit, pat, pit.
Sid can fit. Sam can fit.
Rib can fit.
How will Tim fit?

This is how Tim can fit.

Tim, Sam, Rib, and Sid sit.

Pit, pat, pit, pat, pit.

Lesson 21

Make It Pop!
by Kari Matheson

My Dog Tom
by Amy Miller-Krезelak
illustrated by Amanda Harvey

 WORDS TO KNOW
High-Frequency Words

make
play
them
give
say
new

Vocabulary Reader

Context Cards

Friends
by Olivia Rose

Go Digital

90

Words to Know

Read Together

▶ Read the words.

▶ Talk about the pictures.

make

We make a tower.

play

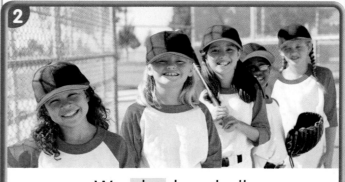
We play baseball.

them

I like to hear them play music.

give

Music teachers give lessons.

say

We say the pledge to the flag.

new

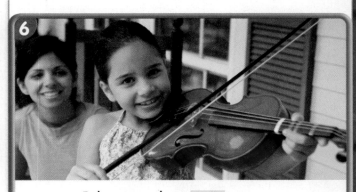

I learned a new song.

Choose one word.
Use it in a sentence.

Your Turn

Talk About It!

How do musicians work together to make music? Talk about it with a partner.

Write About It!

Draw and write about your favorite instrument or musician in the **Big Book.**

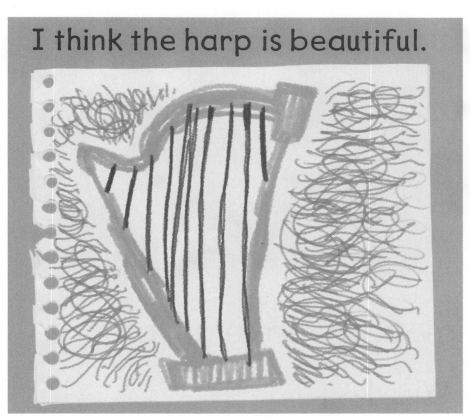

I think the harp is beautiful.

Make It Pop!

by Kari Matheson

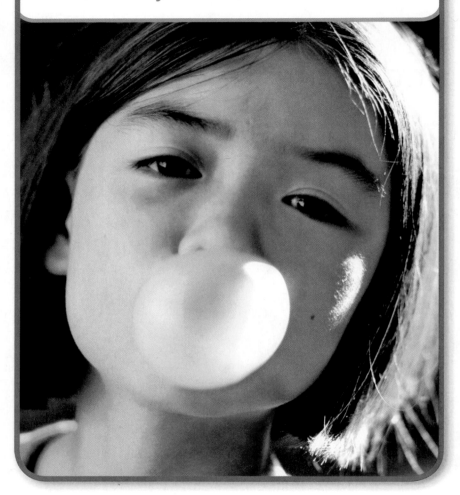

Mim can make it big.
It will pop.

Tom can make it big.
Pop it, Tom!   Pop it!

Dot and Pat play with them.
Pop it, Dot!
Pop it, Pat!

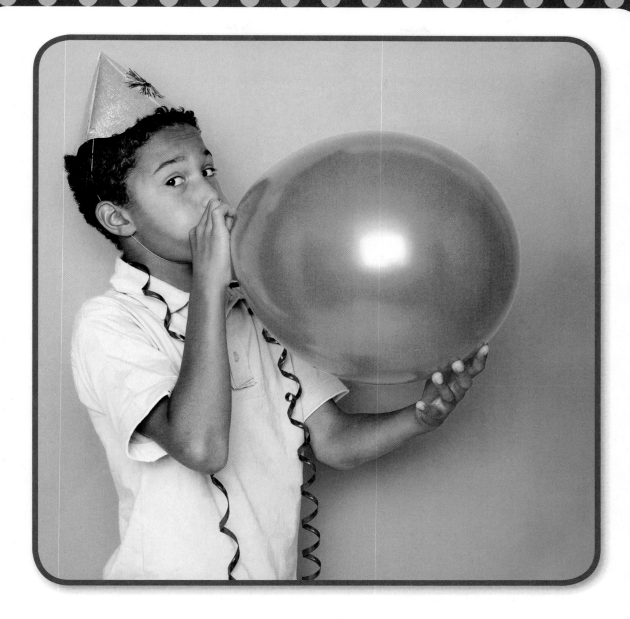

Cam can make it pop.
Pop it, Cam!
Pop it! Pop it!

Pam can make it pop!
Pop it, Pam!
Pop it!   Pop it!

Rob can make it big.
Will it pop, Rob?
I say it will!   Pop it!

My Dog Tom

by Amy Miller-Krezelak

illustrated by Amanda Harvey

Tom is my new dog.
Tom can sit with me.
I can give Tom a pat.

Tom can nap on this pad.

The pad is tan.

Nap on your pad, Tom.

Tom can play.
Tom can nip, nip, nip!
Nip it, Tom!

Tom can dig a big pit.
Tom can dig and dig!
Can Tom play tag?

Tom can play tag.
I can tag Tom.
Tom can tag me.

Tom got big!
Tom and I got big.

✓ WORDS TO KNOW
High-Frequency Words

said

good

was

then

ate

could

Vocabulary Reader

Context Cards

Go Digital

106

Words to Know

Read Together

▶ Read the words.

▶ Talk about the pictures.

said

My dad said I could ride my bike.

good

This watermelon tastes good!

was

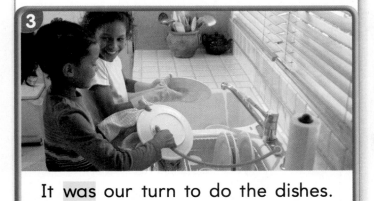

3

It **was** our turn to do the dishes.

then

4

The baby played and **then** clapped her hands.

ate

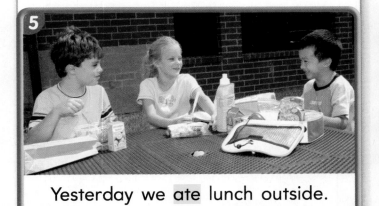

5

Yesterday we **ate** lunch outside.

could

6

Did you know I **could** jump so high?

Choose one word.

Use it in a sentence.

Your Turn

Talk About It!

Think about the **Big Book**. How does Leo change as he grows up? Talk to a friend about it.

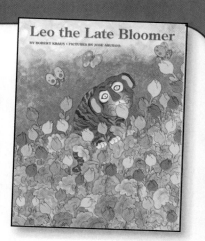

Write About It!

Draw and write about a time you learned to do something new.

I can draw the sun.

109

A Good Job

by Spiro Dantous

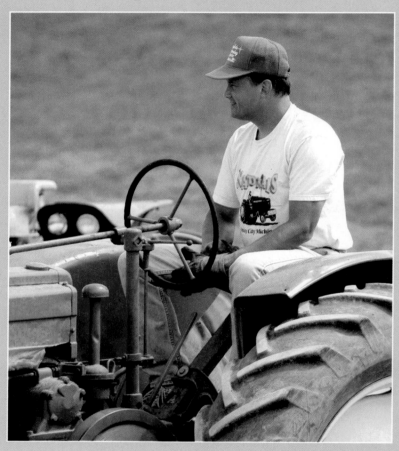

Rod got a job in a rig.
Rod can sit in the rig.

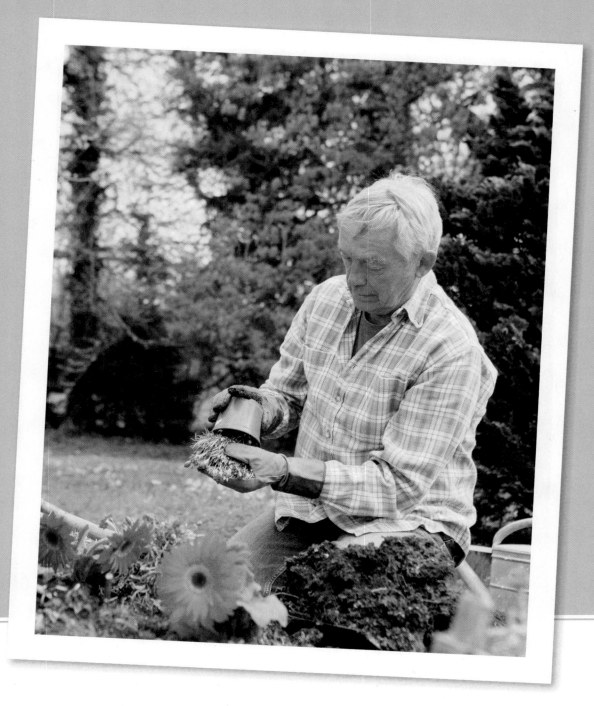

"I got a job," said Jon.
Jon can dig, dig, dig, dig!
Dig, Jon, dig!

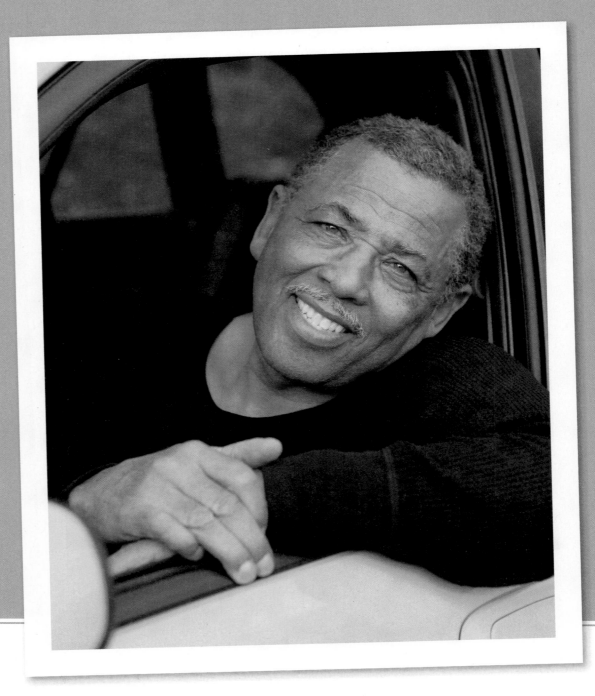

Dom got a job in a cab.
Dom can sit in the cab.

Dot got a job. Dot can tap.
Dot can tap, tap, tap.
Tap it, Dot!

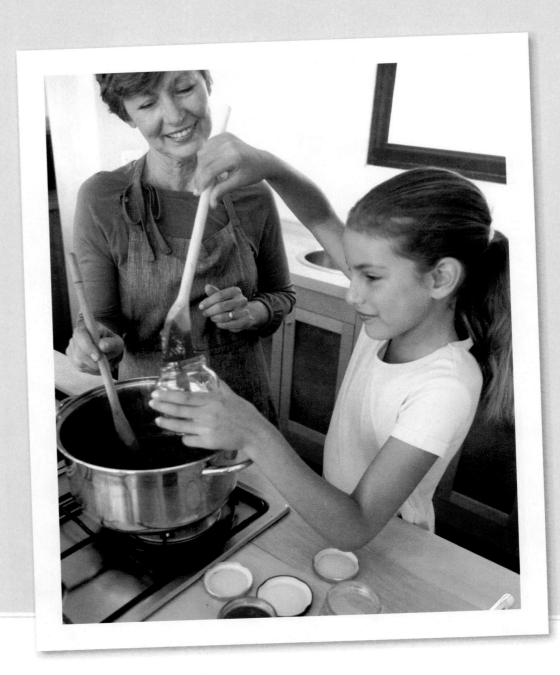

Pam got a job.
Pam could mix jam. Mix it, Pam!
"Then I ate it," said Pam.

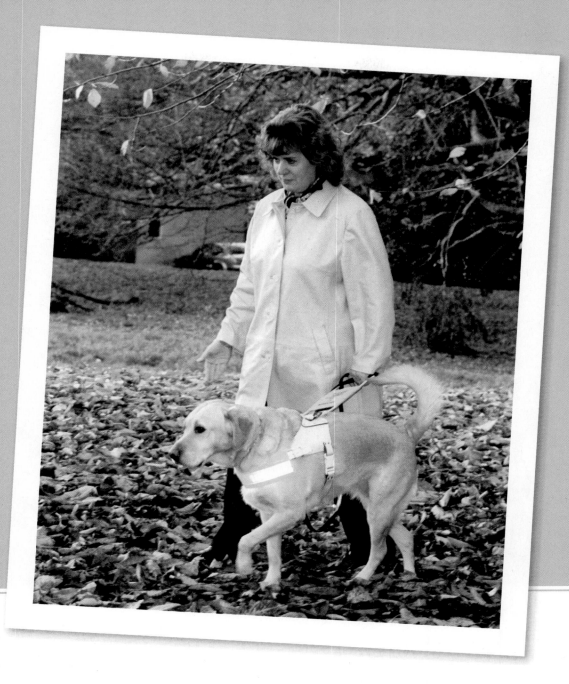

Max Dog got a good job.
Jan can not see. Max can.

Fix It!

by Sue Chang
illustrated by John Berg

The map got a rip in it.
"It was Ox," said Fox.
"Ox did it."

"A job for Ox!" said Dog.
"Fix it! Fix it, Ox. Fix it!"

Then the cap got a rip in it.
"Fox! Fox did it," said Ox.

"Fox can fix it," said Dog.
"Fix it, fix it, fix it, Fox!"

The box got a big rip in it.
"I did it. I did it," said Dog.
"I can fix it, Ox."

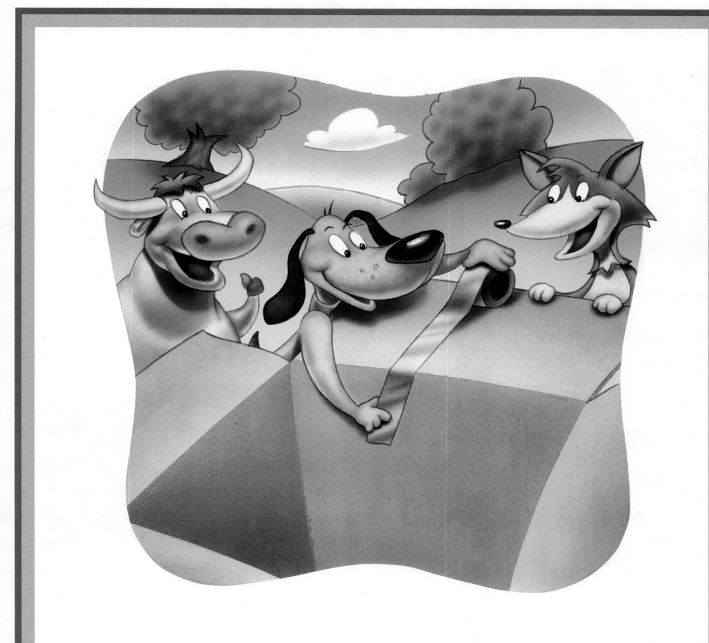

Dog did.
Dog did fix it.
Good job, Dog!

My Pet Dog
by Nina Walker

Ben and Jen
by Debbie Dixon
illustrated by Susan Calitri

✓ **WORDS TO KNOW**
High-Frequency Words

she
all
over
her
when
some

Vocabulary Reader

Context Cards

The Flower
by Nina Schultz
HOUGHTON MIFFLIN

Go Digital

Words to Know

Read Together

▶ Read the words.

▶ Talk about the pictures.

she

She works in the garden.

all

Look at all the colorful flowers!

over

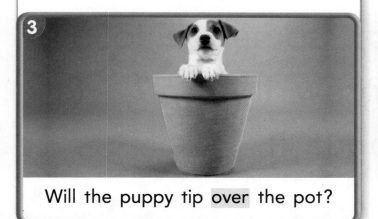

Will the puppy tip over the pot?

her

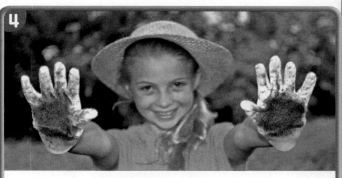

She wore her hat and gloves.

when

They planted the flowers when it was sunny.

some

Please give the plants some water.

Choose one word.
Use it in a sentence.

Your Turn

Talk About It!

What steps can someone follow to plant and grow flowers? Talk to a friend about it.

Zinnia's Flower Garden
·MONICA WELLINGTON·

Write About It!

Draw and write about flowers you would like to grow.

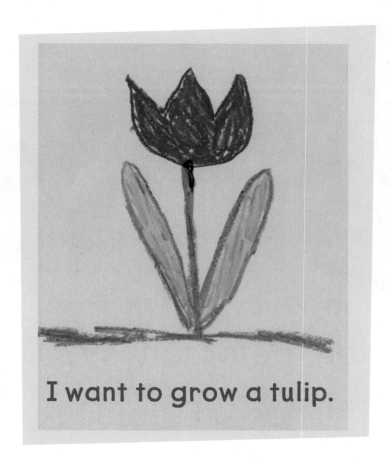

I want to grow a tulip.

Go Digital

My Pet Dog

by Nina Walker

All ten pets can sit.
All ten pets can fit
when they sit.

Ben is her pet dog.
Can Ben get a big pat?

Ted is her pet dog.
Can Ted get a big pat?

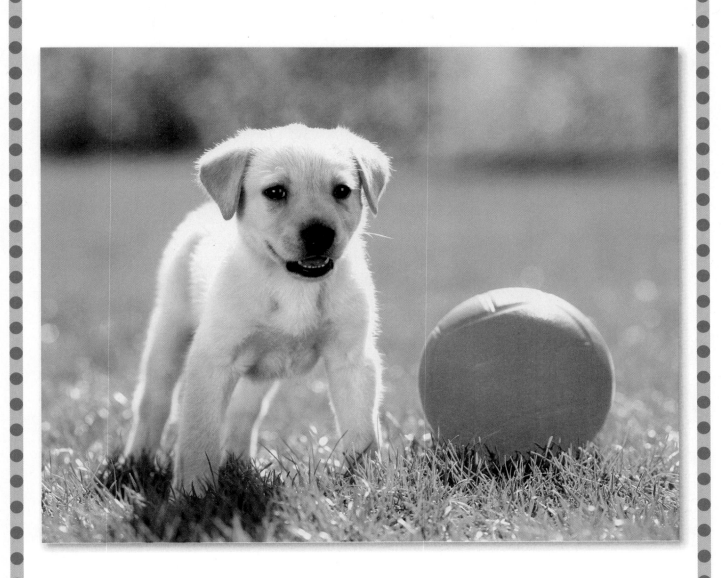

Deb ran, ran, ran.
What did she get?

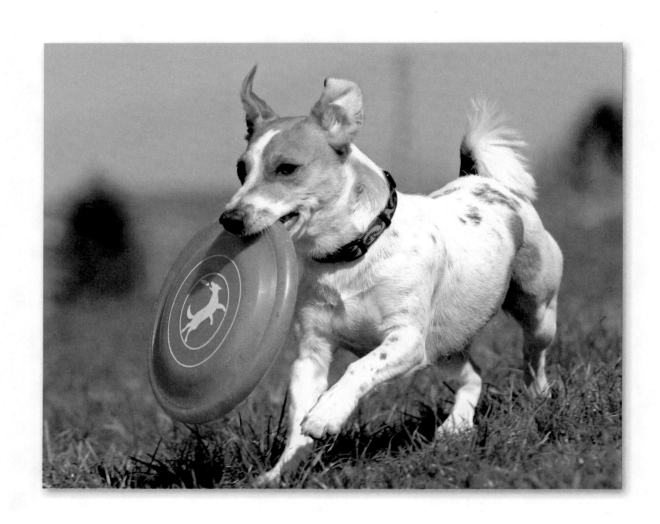

Meg ran over here.
What did she get?

Peg can fit in the bag.
Peg can sit in it.

Ben and Jen

by Debbie Dixon

illustrated by Susan Calitri

"Jen, Jen, Jen!" said Ben.
"I can not get Jen."

"Get a net," said Ed.
Ben can not get Jen.

"Get a box," said Ted.
Ben can not get Jen.

Can Meg get Jen?
She can not get Jen.

Ed and Ted got some men.
Ben and Meg got some men.

"I can get Jen," said Meg.
Meg did it!
Meg did get Jen.

Hog in a Hat
by David McCoy
illustrated by Elizabeth Sayles

Kid Hid
by David McCoy
illustrated by Steven Parton

✓ WORDS TO KNOW
High-Frequency Words

he

no

away

must

by

there

Vocabulary Reader

Context Cards

Words to Know

Read Together

▶ Read the words.

▶ Talk about the pictures.

he

The chameleon is hungry when **he** wakes up.

no

There is **no** chameleon in this tree.

away

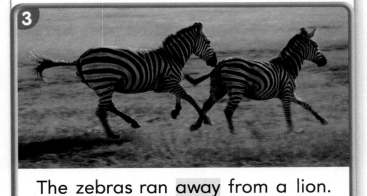

The zebras ran **away** from a lion.

must

This animal **must** hide in the snow.

by

The cheetahs wait side **by** side in the grass.

there

Do you see a fish hiding **there**?

Choose one word.
Use it in a sentence.

Your Turn

Talk About It!

The **Big Book** tells how a chameleon can change colors. How do its colors help it survive? Talk about it with a friend.

Write About It!

Draw and write to share one interesting fact you learned about chameleons.

Go Digital

Hog in a Hat

by David McCoy

illustrated by Elizabeth Sayles

Hog can sit.
He can sit in a big top hat.

Dog can sit.
She can sit in a big red hat.

Cat can sit.

He can sit in a big tan hat.

Hen ran by.
She ran away in a red hat.

Fox can hop.
He can hop in a big hat.

Pig must nap now.
She can nap in a red hat.

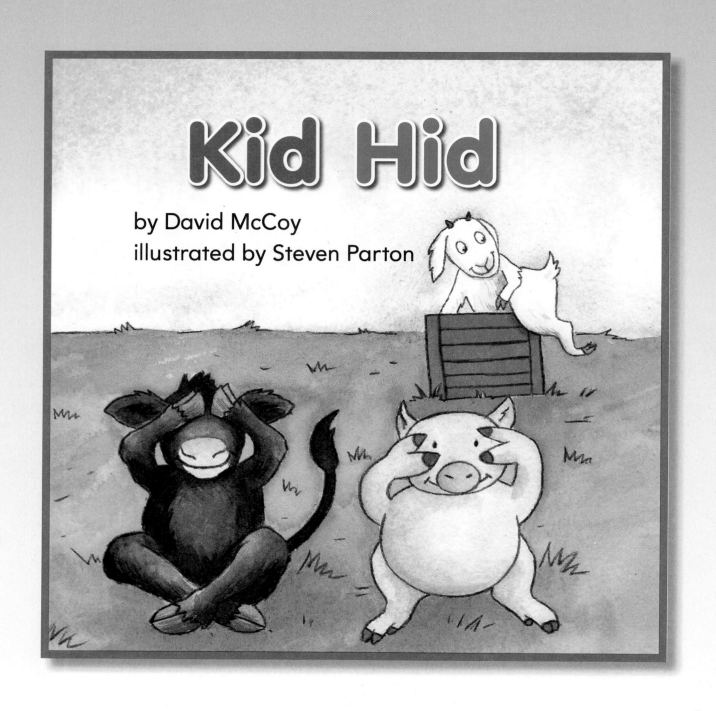

Kid Hid

by David McCoy

illustrated by Steven Parton

Kid hid.

Can he fit in a red box?

No, Kid can not fit in it.
Kim can find him.

Kid hid.

Can he fit in a jet kit?

No, Kid can not fit in there.
Kip can find him.

Can Kid fit in this big pot?
He hid in it.

Kim can not find him!
Kip can not find him!

Six Pigs Hop
by Diana Sheaffer
illustrated Kate Flanagan

Play, Kid, Play
by Franco Denehy
illustrated by Sarah Snow

☑ **WORDS TO KNOW**
High-Frequency Words

play
over
good
said
all
she

Vocabulary Reader

Snack Time
by Molly Chester
HOUGHTON MIFFLIN

Context Cards

We play baseball.

Go Digital

Words to Know

Read Together

▶ You learned these words.

play

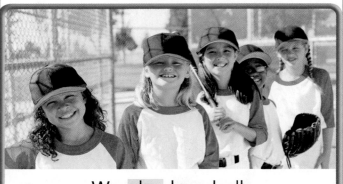

We play baseball.

over

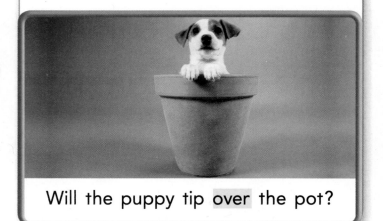

Will the puppy tip over the pot?

good

This watermelon tastes good!

said

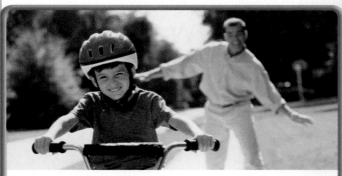

My dad said I could ride my bike.

all

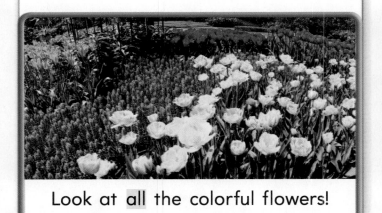

Look at all the colorful flowers!

she

She works in the garden.

Now use each word in a sentence.

Your Turn

Talk About It!

How do people get food from plants? Share your ideas with a partner.

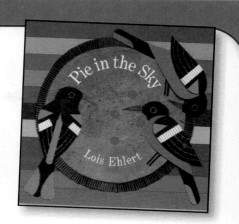

Write About It!

What kind of pie do you like best? Draw and write about it.

Six Pigs Hop

by Diana Sheaffer
illustrated Kate Flanagan

Six pigs sit in a pen.
"Sit, good pigs, sit," said Jen.

Six pigs hop in the pen.
Hop, pigs. Hop, hop, hop.

All six pigs hop and hop.

Hop, pigs, hop.

Six pigs hop over the top.

Six pigs go for a dip.
Dip, pigs.   Dip, dip.
Can six pigs play?

Six pigs can play.

Six pigs can see Jen.

She can see six pigs.

Six pigs can sit.

Six pigs can dig in the pen.

"Dig pigs, dig," said Jen.

Play, Kid, Play

by Franco Denehy

illustrated by Sarah Snow

Dad Fox had a big box.
Dad Fox hid it.

Dad Fox hid the big box.
Can Red Hen find it?
Red Hen did find it.

"It is not for me," said Red Hen.
"It is not.   It is not."

Can Jon Dog find the big
box Dad Fox hid?
Jon Dog did find it.

"It is not for me," said Jon
Dog. "Kid Fox! Kid Fox!
Dad Fox hid this box!"

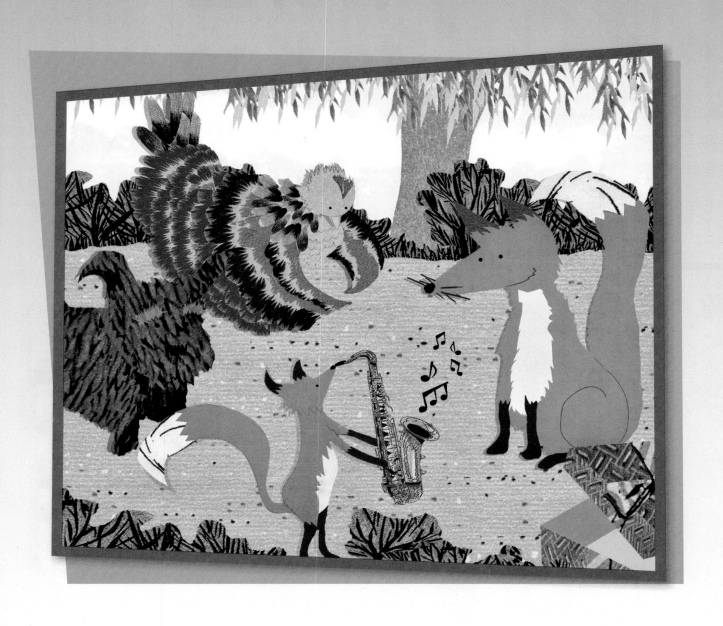

Kid Fox got the big box.
It had a sax in it.
She can play it.

Fun, Fun, Fun
by Bonnie Whitmark

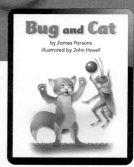

Bug and Cat
by James Parsons
illustrated by John Hovell

✓ WORDS TO KNOW
High-Frequency Words

down

do

went

only

little

just

Vocabulary Reader

I Can!
by Brady Hayes
HOUGHTON MIFFLIN

Context Cards

Go Digital

Words to Know

Read Together

▶ Read the words.

▶ Talk about the pictures.

down

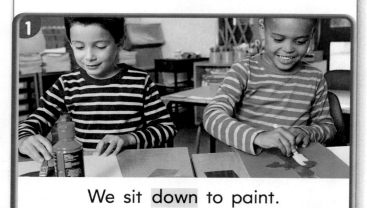

We sit **down** to paint.

do

A dog can **do** lots of tricks.

went

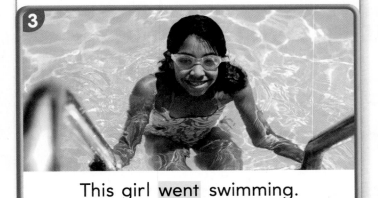

This girl **went** swimming.

only

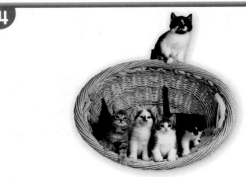

Only one kitten is out of the basket.

little

The **little** bunny is eating a carrot.

just

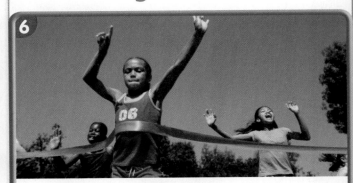

The girl **just** won the race.

Choose one word.
Use it in a sentence.

Your Turn

Talk About It!

In the **Big Book**, Kitten tries very hard to get a bowl of milk. Why is it important to try hard? Share your ideas with a partner.

Write About It!

What was your favorite part of the story? Draw and write about it.

173

Fun, Fun, Fun

by Bonnie Whitmark

Kit is in the bag.
Kit has fun in a bag.

What do little pups do for fun?
Pups can tug, tug, tug.

Some pups just run, run, run.
It is fun to run, run, run.

Some dogs only dig for fun.
This big dog dug, dug, dug down.

Big dogs can run, run, run.
It is fun to run, run, run.

This big cat ran up.

It went up, up, up.

Bug and Cat

by James Parsons
illustrated by John Hovell

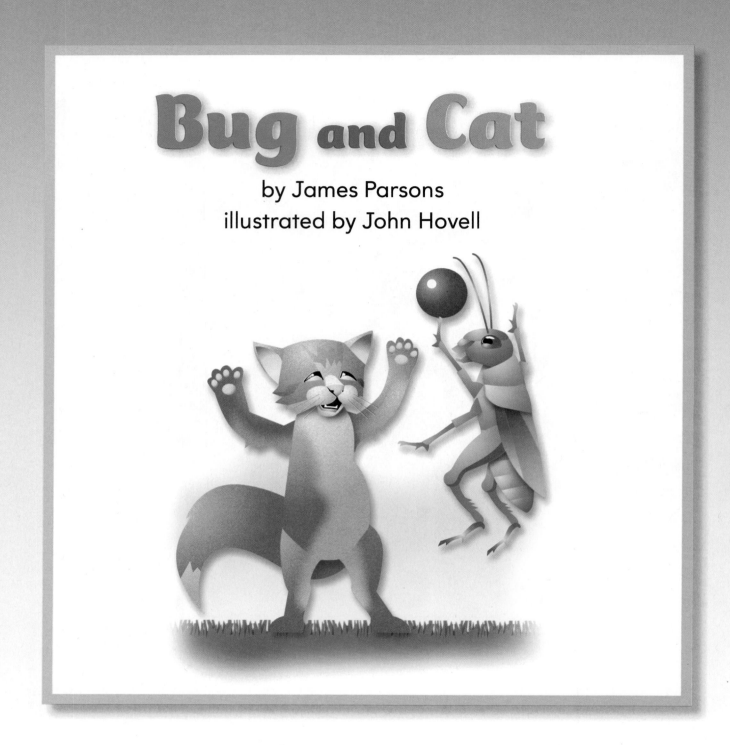

Bug and Cat can play.
It is fun, fun, fun!

Bug can hop up and down.
Hop, hop, hop. Fun, fun, fun.

Cat can hit this for fun.
Rum, tum, tum! Rum, tum!

Bug can hum. Cat can hum.
Hum, Bug. Hum, Cat.

Bug can sit on a rug.
Cat can sit on a rug.

Do Bug and Cat run?
Bug and Cat run, run, run!

Win a Cup!
by Todd Turriro
illustrated by Marilyn Janovitz

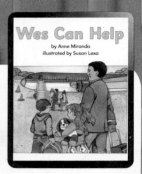

Wes Can Help
by Anne Miranda
illustrated by Susan Lexa

✓ WORDS TO KNOW
High-Frequency Words

have

help

one

every

ask

walk

Vocabulary Reader

Let's Have Fun!
by Marty James

Context Cards

Go Digital

Words to Know

Read Together

▶ Read the words.

▶ Talk about the pictures.

have

I have one baby brother.

help

I help my mom draw.

one

This is the one I want.

every

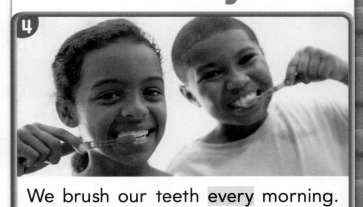

We brush our teeth every morning.

ask

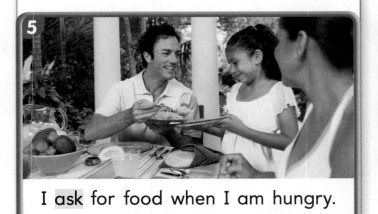

I ask for food when I am hungry.

walk

We walk in the park.

Choose one word.
Use it in a sentence.

Your Turn

Talk About It!

What is it like to be the youngest in a family? How does the youngest girl in the **Big Book** feel? Talk to a friend about it.

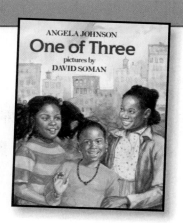

Write About It!

The girl in the story does many things. Draw and write about something she does that you would like to do.

Win a Cup!

by Todd Turriro

illustrated by Marilyn Janovitz

Meg can run, run, run!
Meg can win a big cup.

Ken can hit and run.
Ken can win a big cup.

Pam can hit every one down.
Pam can win a big cup.

Wes can help Lon.
Lon can help Wes win.

Wes can win a big cup!
Lon can win a big cup!

We all have a cup.

Wes Can Help

by Anne Miranda

illustrated by Susan Lexa

Len and Meg walk up to a big jet.
Len and Meg will have fun.

Wes led Len. Len can sit.
Wes led Meg. Meg can sit.

Len will ask Wes for help.
Wes got the big bag up.

Wes got Len a hot dog.
Wes got Meg a sub.

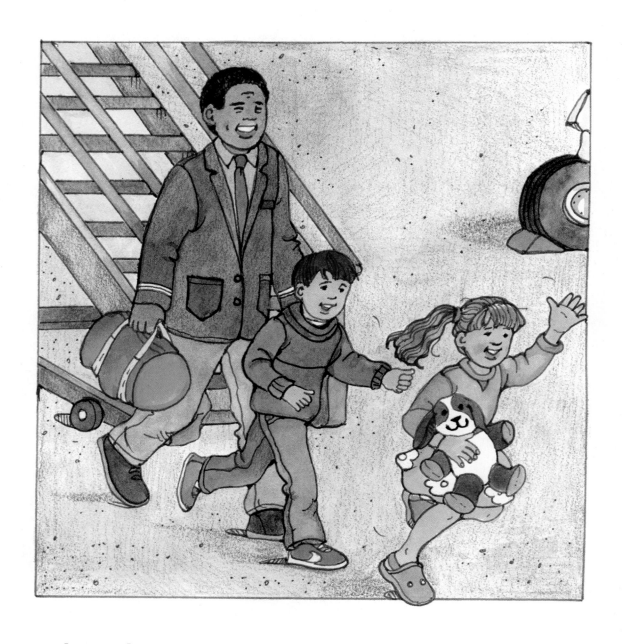

The big jet is down.
Len can run.   Meg can run.

Len had fun. Meg had fun.
Wes had fun.

Vet on a Job!
by Anne Miranda

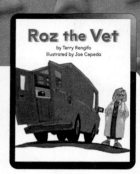

Roz the Vet
by Terry Rengifo
illustrated by Joe Cepeda

✓ WORDS TO KNOW
High-Frequency Words

look
out
very
their
saw
put

Vocabulary Reader

Context Cards

Words to Know

▶ Read the words.

▶ Talk about the pictures.

look

We look at the art.

out

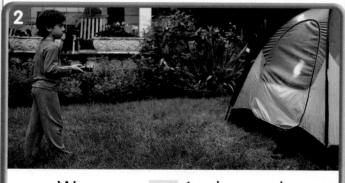

We camp out in the yard.

very

I play the piano very well.

their

They use their hands to play this game.

saw

The boy saw the toys.

put

She put the spoons away.

Choose one word.
Use it in a sentence.

Your Turn

Talk About It!

Why is it important to help your friends? Share your ideas with a partner.

Write About It!

Think about things that Curious George does in the **Big Book** story. Draw and write about something he does.

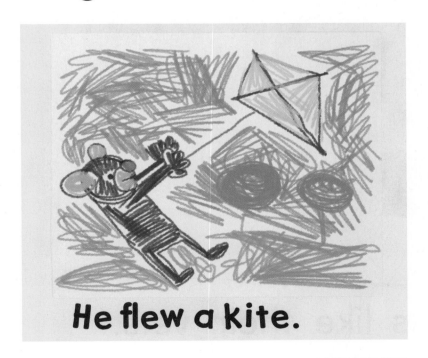

He flew a kite.

Vet on a Job!

by Anne Miranda

Pets like their vets.
Vets can help pets.

Dot the vet saw Bud.
Dot fed Bud. Sip it, Bud.

Val the vet can look at Vin.
Vin can run now.

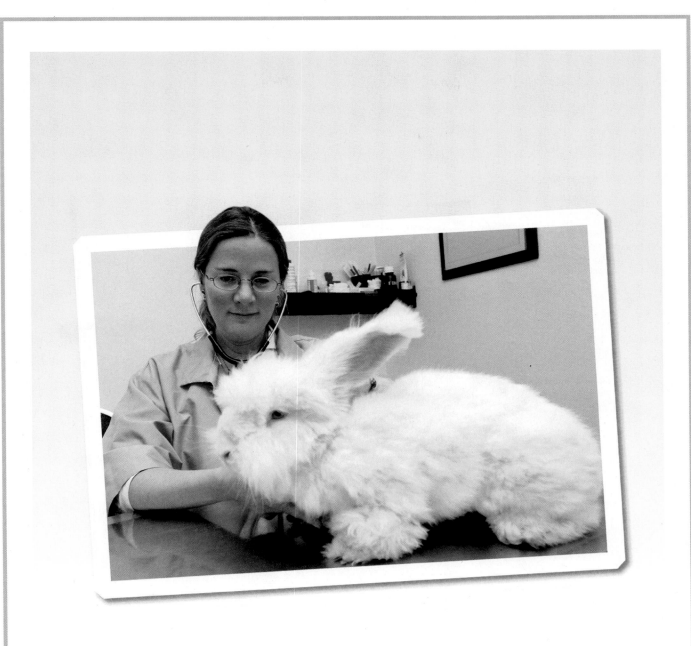

Zeb is very sad.

Zeb can not hop.

Bev the vet can look at Zeb.

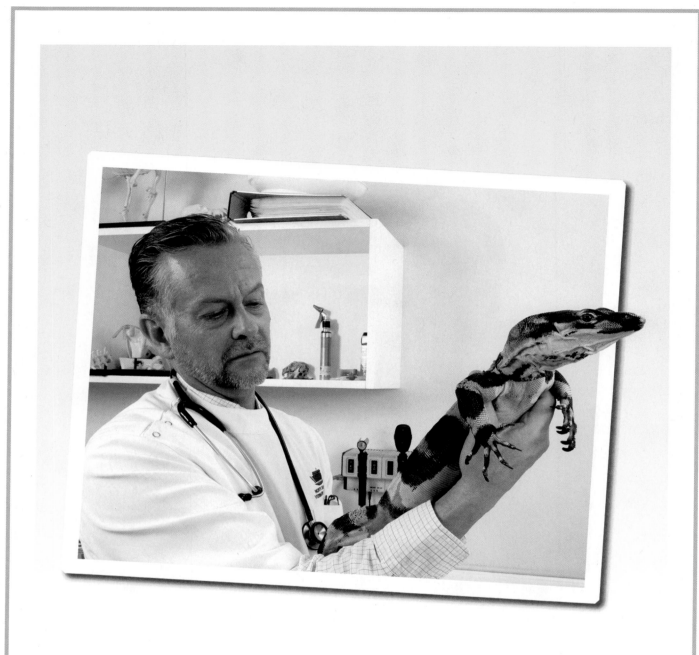

Vic the vet can look at Zip.
Zip can not get out.

Lil the vet can look at Sam.
Lil can pet Sam.

Roz the Vet

by Terry Rengifo

illustrated by Joe Cepeda

Roz the vet can help a pet!
Roz can zip in her red van.

Roz can look at a pet pig.
Roz fed it. Sip it, little pig.

Roz the vet can help a pet!
Roz can zip in her red van.

Vic had a bad cut.
Roz put Vic in the van.
Roz can fix it, Vic!

Tab Cat got out.   Tab ran up.
Tab had fun.   Tab can not get down.

Tab saw Roz.

Roz can get Tab.

Not Yet
by Nancy Spencer

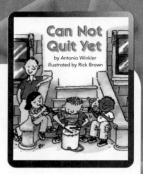
Can Not Quit Yet
by Antonio Winkler
illustrated by Rick Brown

✓ WORDS TO KNOW
High-Frequency Words

off

take

our

day

too

show

Vocabulary Reader

Context Cards

Go Digital

Words to Know

Read Together

▸ Read the words.

▸ Talk about the pictures.

off

We get **off** the bus.

take

We **take** turns.

our

We raise our hands.

day

We show the weather for each day.

too

We draw houses.
We draw people, too.

show

We show our pictures.

Choose one word.
Use it in a sentence.

Your Turn

Read Together

Talk About It!

What did you learn in kindergarten? Talk about it with a partner.

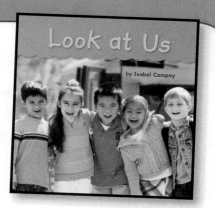

Write About It!

What can you do now that you couldn't do before kindergarten? Draw and write about it.

Not Yet

by Nancy Spencer

Cat, do not get up yet!
Nap on the little red mat.

Dog, do not get up yet!
Nap on the big rug all day.

Hen, do not get up yet!
Nap in the hen box.

Pig, do not get up yet!
Nap in the pig pen.

Fox, do not get up yet!
Nap in the fox den.

Bat, get up! Bat, take off!
Bats only quit at sun up!

Can Not Quit Yet

by Antonio Winkler
illustrated by Rick Brown

Yes, yes! Ben can hit it.
Ben hit the tub, rum tum!

Rum, tum, tum!
Show us how to do it, Ben.

Yes, yes! Tim can dig.
Tim can dig and dig.

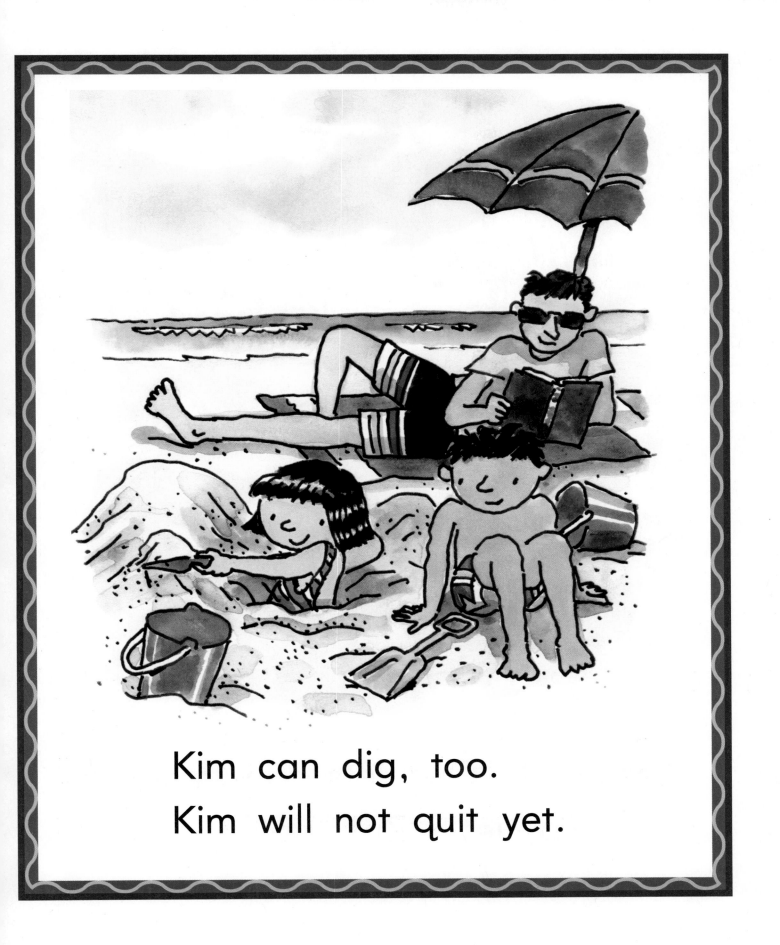

Kim can dig, too.
Kim will not quit yet.

Yes, yes! Our jets can take off.
Zip, zip, jet! Zip, zip!

It can zip, zip, zip.
Meg can not quit yet.

WORDS TO KNOW
High-Frequency Words

down
ask
help
walk
look
show

Vocabulary Reader

Context Cards

Go Digital

Words to Know

Read Together

▶ You learned these words.

down

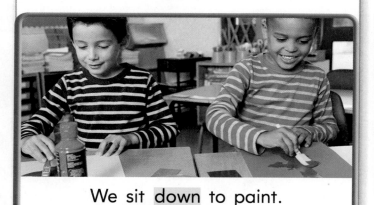

We sit down to paint.

ask

I ask for food when I am hungry.

help

I **help** my mom draw.

walk

We **walk** in the park.

look

We **look** at the art.

show

We **show** our pictures.

Now use each word in
a sentence.

Your Turn

Talk About It!

What can you do to be a good friend? Share ideas with a partner.

my WriteSmart

Write About It!

Write about your favorite part of the story.

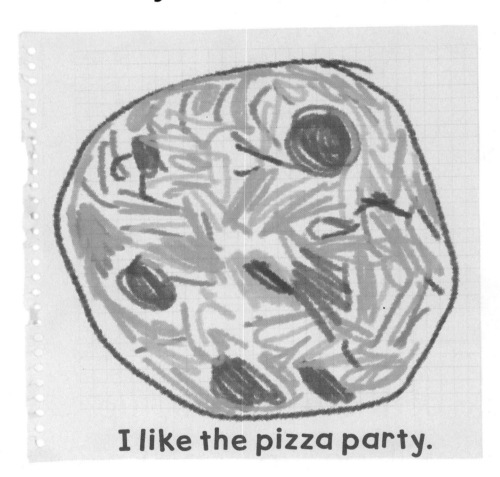

I like the pizza party.

 Go Digital

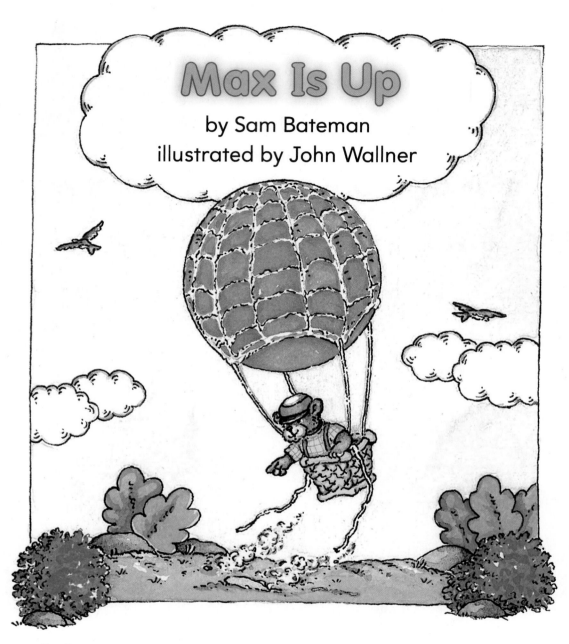

Max Is Up

by Sam Bateman

illustrated by John Wallner

Max can go up, up, up.
Max will go up, up, up.

Max is up.

Max can not get down.

"Help!" said Max.

Bud ran.

Can Bud get Max down?

Look!   Bud can not get Max.

Tom ran. Can Tom get Max?
Look! Tom can not get Max.
Ask Big Ben to help us.

Big Ben can tug, tug, tug.
Will Max get down?
Tug, Big Ben, tug!
Will Max get down?

Yes. He did!
Big Ben got Max down.

A Fun Job

by Priscilla Banab

illustrated by Jeff Mack

Ted has a job.
Deb has a job.

"Find nuts," said Mom.
"Get nuts. Get lots of nuts."
Ted and Deb walk to get nuts.

Ted got nuts. Deb got nuts.
It is a fun job to get nuts.
It is fun, fun, fun.

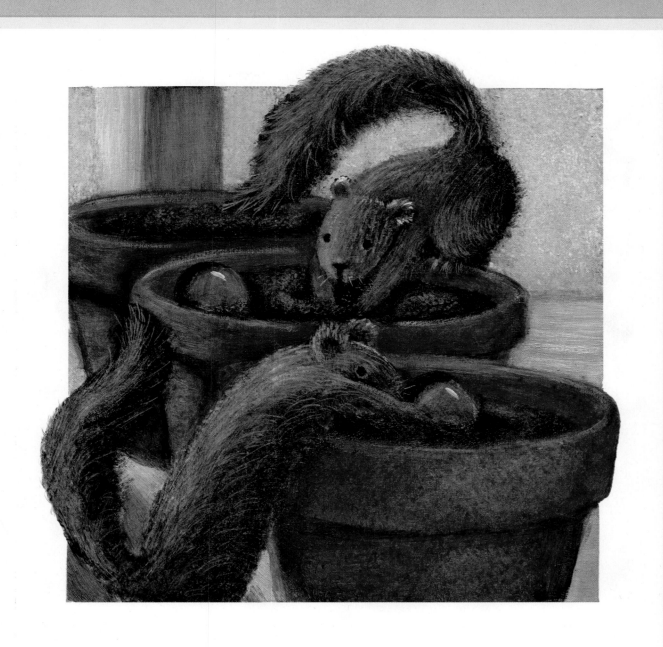

Ted can show Deb what to do.
Ted hid nuts in pots.
Deb hid nuts in pots.

Look at the pots.
Can Ted and Deb see nuts?
No, Ted and Deb can not.

Ted hid nuts in pots.
Deb hid nuts in pots.
What is in the pots now?

Fast Track

Long *i, o, e* Words

so	me	I	We

1. _____ am at bat.

2. _____ can play.

3. It is _____ hot!

4. Look at _____ !

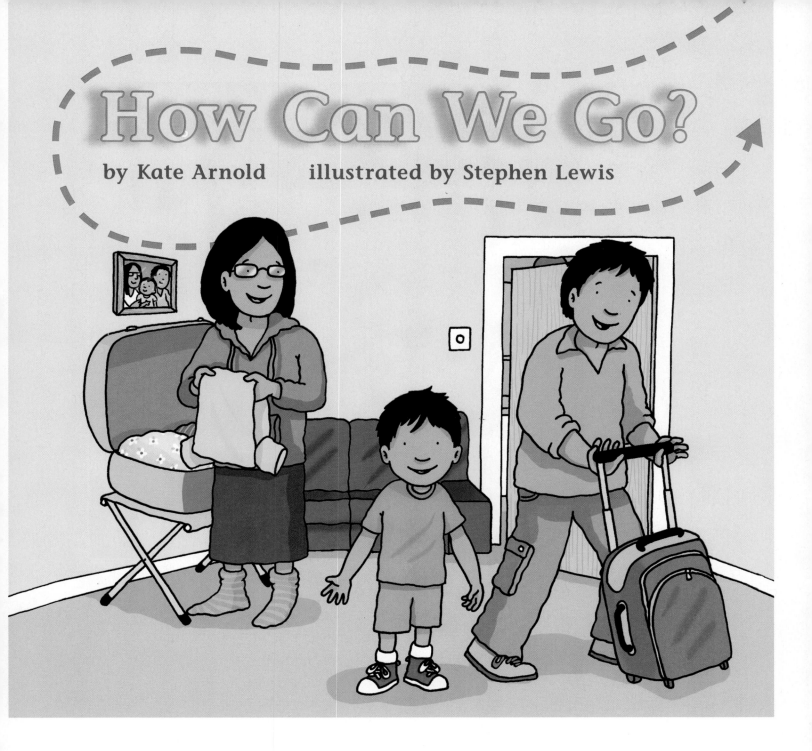

How Can We Go?

by Kate Arnold   illustrated by Stephen Lewis

I am Tim. I can go.
Mom and Dad will go with me.
How can we go?
What will we see?

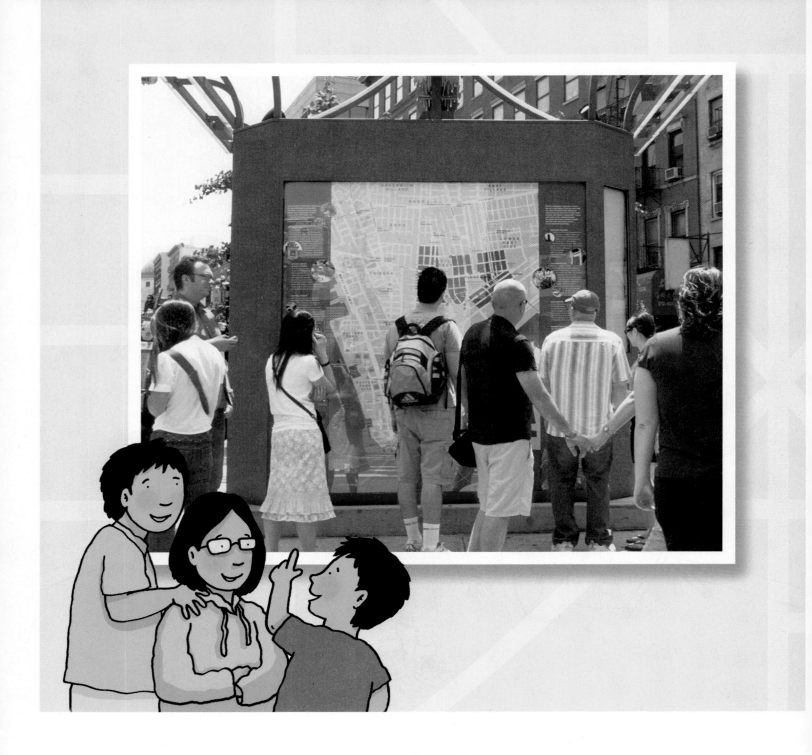

We can find a map.
It will help us.
We can go and go.
We will see a lot.

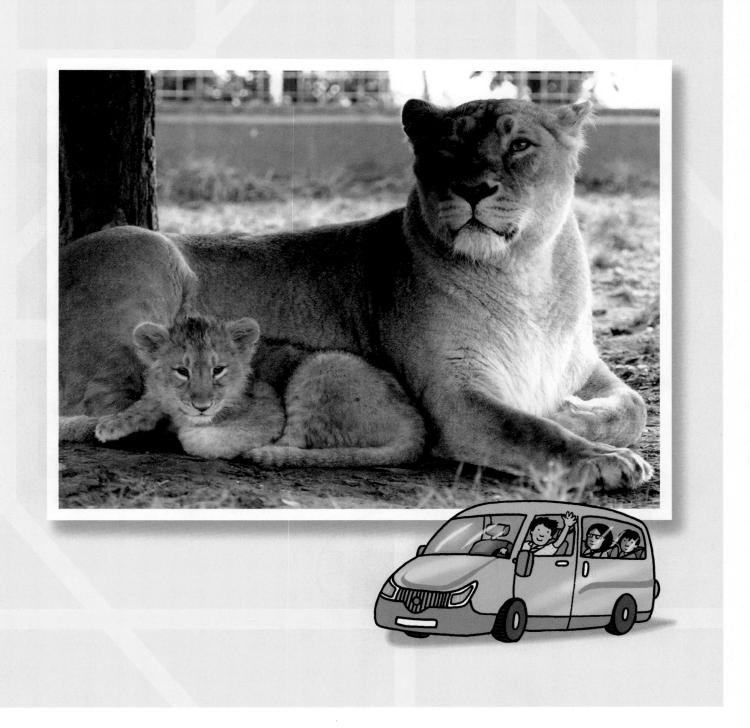

We can go in a van.
We will see a lot of big cats.
Will we see a cub? Yes!

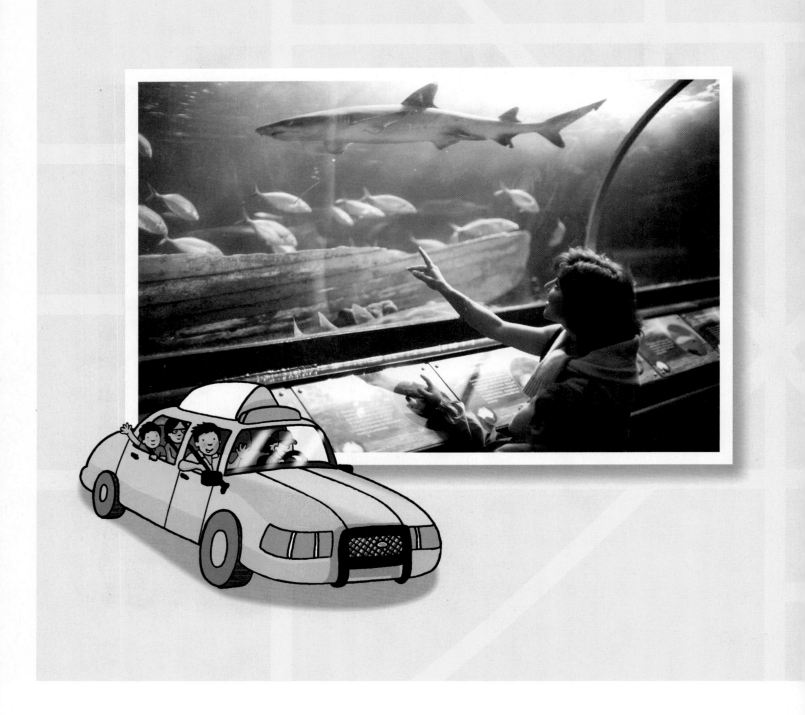

We can go in a cab.
We will see a big fin.
Will we get wet? No!

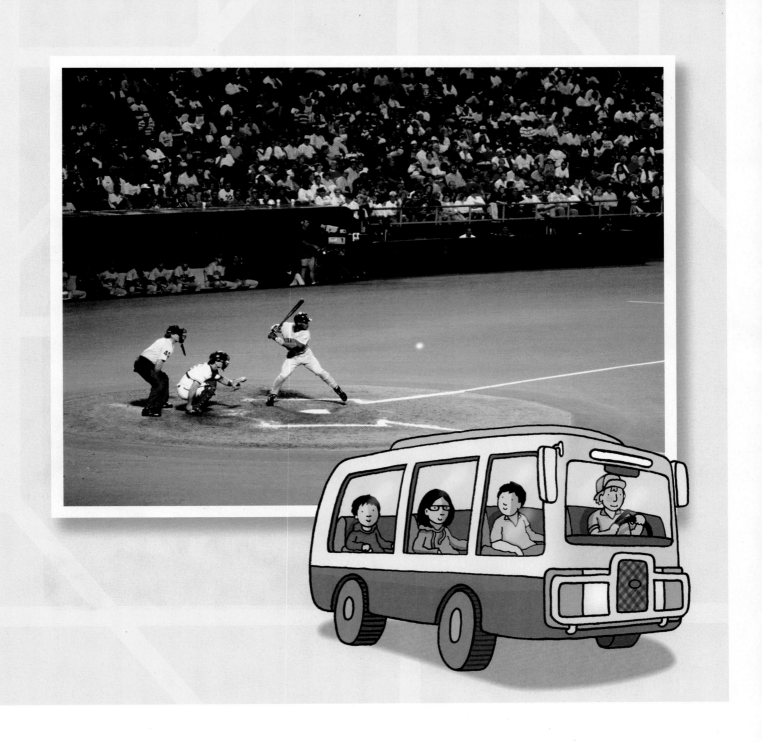

We can go on a bus.
We will see a man at bat.
Will he get a hit?
Yes! Go! Go! Go!

We can go on a jet.
We will see a lot.
It will be so fun!

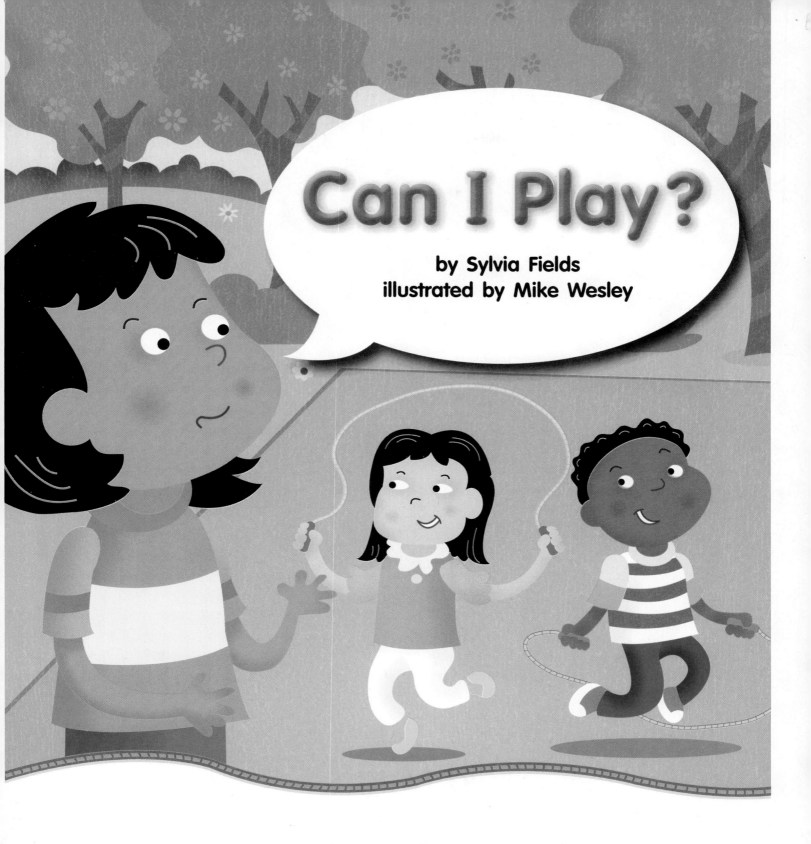

Can I Play?

by Sylvia Fields
illustrated by Mike Wesley

"Hi," said Jan.
"Can I play?"

"Hi," said Meg.
"Yes, come and play.
I go up and down like this."

"Hi," said Tim. "Do it like this.
Can you do it?"
"No," said Jan. "I can not."

"I will help," said Meg.
"We can do this."

"Look at me!" said Jan.
"I can go up and down now.
I can play."

"Hi," said Ben. "Can I play?"
"Hi," said Jan.
"Yes, we can all play now!"

tape

gate

cane

rake

game

kite   kit

pine   pin

dim   dime

time   Tim

Get Set! Dive!

by Ben Ward
illustrated by Darcia Labrosse

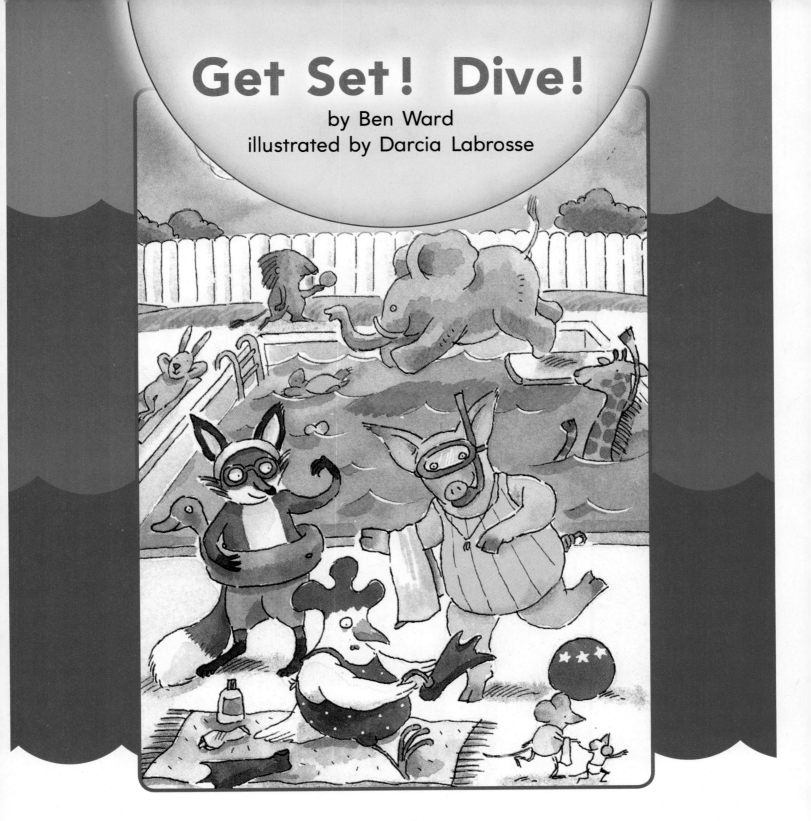

"Come," said Fox.
"We can dive.
We can make a big wave."

Can Hen dive?

Get set! Dive! Hen can do it!

Hen can make a big wave.

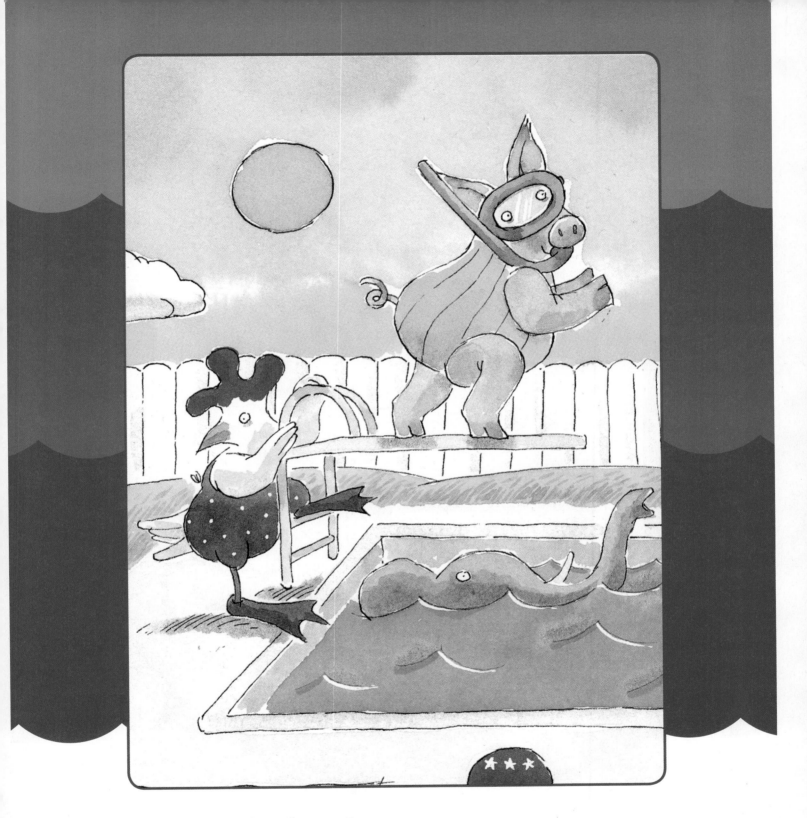

Can Pig dive?

Get set! Dive! Pig can do it!

Pig can make a big wave.

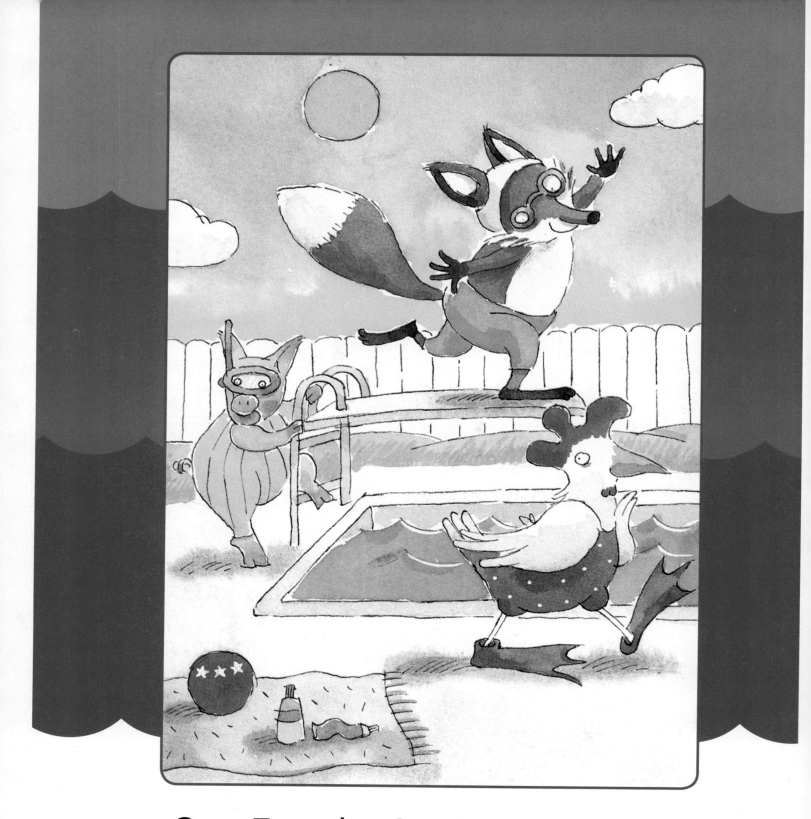

Can Fox dive?

Get set! Dive! Fox can do it!

"This is fun," said Fox.

"Look!" said Pig.
"We can play a game.
We will get wet."

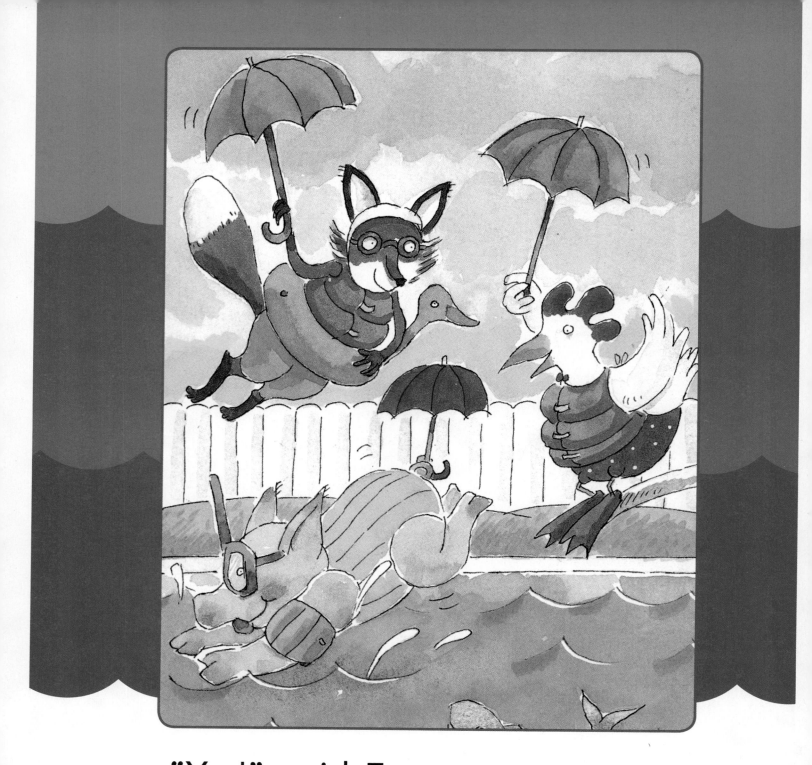

"Yes!" said Fox.
"It is time to play.
We will make a fine wave."
Look out!

Long *o* Words

1   tote   tot

2   rod   rode

3   not   note

Take Rex to the vet.

4   robe   Rob

273

Long *u* Words

June   dune   tube   cubes

Luke, June, and Rose

by Denise Daniels

illustrated by Diane Palmisciano

"Rose is in the mud!" said Luke.
"This is bad!" said June.

Rose will get in the tub.
June will use the hose.
"It will be fun, Rose!" said Luke.

"You got me!" said Luke.

"Is this a joke?"

"No," said June.

"The hose will not go down."

"Look, no mud!" said Luke.
Luke and June do a good job.

"No, Rose!" said Luke.
"You will get June wet!"

"Rose is cute," said June.

"Yes, she is!" said Luke.

"She is a good dog," said Mom.

"She can have a big bone."

Photo Credits

Placement Key: (r) right, (l) left, (c) center, (t) top, (b) bottom, (bg) background

Illustration